NEXT LEVEL STUDENT SUCCESS

Practical Ways to Achieve Success in
School and in Life.

DENNARD MITCHELL

Next Level Student Success

Cover Photography by Michael Warning

Printed in the United States of America

ISBN: 978-0-578-66314-2

NL Publishing

TABLE OF CONTENTS

INTRODUCTION

Finally! If you're reading this book, I did it! I finally completed the book. For years, I had the idea to write a book that would help students, and for years I allowed excuses to derail me. I'm excited to share a book that all students can identify with.

Next Level Student Success is a gold mine for students with the aspirations to take their academic and personal lives to the Next Level. What you are about to read in the following pages is very practical, and very powerful once applied.

Thank you for taking the time to invest in your Success!

"Opportunities don't happen. You create them."

-- Chris Grosser

1

NEXT LEVEL VISION

Do you have a vision? The thought probably streaming through your mind is, of course, I have a vision, which is what is giving me the ability to read this book. However, when I pose the question - do you have a vision? - I'm not referring to physical sight. Rather, I am alluding to having the ability to see beyond where you are right now.

That is what vision is all about. Do you or have you set a plan for your school experience? Better yet, have you developed a plan for life after school? If not, it's A-Okay. Over the course of this book and chapter(s), I will dive into what it takes to not only develop a vision but to move in the *direction* of that vision.

"I find that the harder I work, the more luck I seem to have."

-- Thomas Jefferson

Before I proceed, I want you to know what the term vision means precisely. According to Dictionary.com, vision means a vivid, imaginative conception or anticipation.

My friends, having a vision is so important. It is one of the fundamental elements of success. And why is that so? Because vision allows you to see and visualize internally what you want to achieve externally. One key principle that still and will always stay true is, whatever you see on the inside is going to show itself on the outside. This includes school and any other endeavors that you chose to pursue. It is far greater to have a vision without sight than to have sight without vision! If you don't believe me, then take a look at seemingly successful individuals without having the use of their physical sight.

Individuals such as Helen Keller, Ray Charles, Andrea Bocelli, Stevie Wonder, or maybe even someone you know personally. What allowed these individuals to achieve levels of success and even greatness? I would argue that it was their ability to see on the inside that gave them success on the outside. Although you might possess your physical sight, the same principle holds true for you. You must develop a vision if you have desires and aspirations of achieving great things in school and beyond.

"The ones who are crazy enough to think they can change the world are the ones that do."

-- Anonymous

Over the next few pages, I want to ask you some questions that would better assist you in developing your vision for the future. Take a moment to answer these questions in great detail.

What vision do you see for yourself while in school?

_____

_____

_____

_____

_____

_____

_____

What vision do you see for yourself after Graduating?

_____

_____

_____

_____

_____

_____

_____

"All progress takes place outside the comfort zone."

-- Michael John Bobak

What do you see yourself achieving while in school?

_____

_____

_____

_____

_____

_____

_____

Where do you see yourself five years from now?

_____

_____

_____

_____

_____

_____

_____

"The only limit to our realization of tomorrow will be our doubts of today."

-- Franklin D. Roosevelt

Where do you see yourself 10 years from now?

_____

_____

_____

_____

_____

_____

_____

_____

When you view yourself, what do you see or believe?

_____

_____

_____

_____

_____

_____

_____

_____

"The way to get started is to quit talking and begin doing."

-- Walt Disney

If you could achieve anything, what would it be?

_____

_____

_____

_____

_____

_____

_____

_____

What would you attempt to achieve if you knew there was no possible way that you could fail?

_____

_____

_____

_____

_____

_____

_____

_____

*"The successful warrior is the average man,
with laser-like focus."*

-- Bruce Lee

Great! Now, based on your responses and answers to the questions above, you should have developed a vision or a picture of how your future can look. This is the first step to moving in the direction of your greatness. Notice that I said, '*first* step' and not the only step. There are certainly more steps to take and more blocks to put into place to get you to where you want to be academically, professionally, and personally.

Also, as you progress and grow, so will your vision. Meaning the more you go, the more you grow. So, your vision will continue to grow and expand as you travel along your journey throughout life. However, it will not grow if you have not developed or even had the slightest idea that you have a vision. By answering the questions above, you have identified pieces of your future that serve as part of your vision.

Over the next nine chapters, you will receive information and concepts that can further help you craft your vision. Let's go!!!

"If you fail to plan, you are planning to fail."

-Benjamin Franklin

2

NEXT LEVEL GOAL SETTING

Throughout this book, you will find me referring to the importance of setting goals. Consequently, goal setting is so vital that I've decided to write an entire chapter on the topic.

What are goals? You can look up the term goals and find several different definitions or meanings. I like to think of goals as a measuring device—something to aim, strive, or shoot for.

In addition to having goals for yourself, I believe it's vitally important to write these goals down. Writing them down gets them out of your head and eliminates the chance of forgetting them. I recommend you jot your goals down in either your phone, computer, school planner, your favorite notebook, or journal —somewhere you can *always* see them. The more you see and review your goals, the more they will be fresh and in the forefront of your mind. The first step in writing goals is to identify the areas in which you want to set goals. Examples include social, academics, fitness, etc.

"The difference between who you are and who you want to be is what you do."

-- Unknown

Take a moment to jot down the areas in which you would like to set goals.

1. _____

2. _____

3. _____

4. _____

5. _____

6. _____

7. _____

GOOD JOB!

Now that you have identified all the areas in which you want to set goals, the next step is to focus on each area and write out the goals in great detail. *The more detailed you are, the better the chance you have at accomplishing them.* Each goal you write down **must be specific, measurable, attainable, realistic, and timely.**

"I failed my way to success."

-- Thomas Edison

Specific

When I say your goals should be specific, I mean distinctly to the point. A student can say that they want to pass their math class, which is an okay statement, but it's much too broad.

On the other hand, that same student can say that they want to pass their math class with an "A" for their final grade. This certainly turns the broad statement into a specific one, giving you an outcome to work towards. Furthermore, this statement also allows the student to have a better drive and focus.

Once the student is focused on precisely what he or she wants, now they can formulate a game plan to achieve that "A" in their math class.

Having a goal is like knowing the end result. Once you have identified the end result, you can break it down and develop a plan of action. In this particular case, the student's goal/end result is to pass their math class with an "A." Now let's break it down into chunks. We know that there are a certain number of weeks in a semester per school year. This student will achieve their goal one week at a time. Breaking the ultimate goal into smaller ones and focusing on one semester at a time. Specific goals help you zoom in on your target.

"The only place where success comes before work is in the dictionary."

-- Vince Lombardi

Measurable

While in pursuit of hitting your goals, it is important that you see how you measure up to where you are versus where you want to go. A lot of students set goals, but they never measure their progress. Make sure you have a way to keep track of your results.

Let's refer back to the example of the student with the goal to pass their math class with an "A." They can keep track of their progress through class assignments and tests. Calculating grades earned from the class assignments and tests should give the student a good idea of how close to or far away they are from hitting their goal.

Attainable

In addition to your goals being specific and measurable, they must also be attainable. In other words, you must set goals that do not seem too farfetched that you get tired in the process. What good is having a goal that seems too distant to achieve? That's the purpose of what I talked about in the previous section regarding breaking your goals down into chunks or smaller segments.

"Success is not the absence of failure; it's the persistence through failure."

– Aisha Tyler

The achievement of short-term goals would keep you pumped and motivated to continue until you achieve the ultimate goal. Now, I'm not suggesting that the goals you set should be easy because that would certainly be a false statement. However, you want to set goals that are reachable and attainable within the time frame you've allocated for that particular goal.

For example, writing 150 pages was my goal for this book. Now, it would have been foolish for me to think that I'd write the book in one day or even one week. Is it possible? Absolutely! With extreme focus, commitment, and determination.

However, I knew that it would take me longer than that, so I decided to set a series of attainable goals. The goal was to write three pages a day. This was certainly something I could achieve daily. I knew that if I wrote three pages a day, I would ultimately get to 150 pages in approximately 50 days. Do you see how short-term goals can help you stay focused and motivated to continue?

"Success is achieved and maintained by those who try and keep trying."

– W. Clement Stone

Realistic

DREAM BIG! From this point forward, I encourage you to dream the biggest dreams possible. There is absolutely nothing wrong with dreaming big, just as long as the dreams/goals are realistic. The root word of realistic is "real." Setting realistic goals makes them real and alive.

Here is a list of realistic goals to further explain this part of goal setting.

Examples of Realistic Goals

➢ Getting an "A" in your class

➢ Getting straight A's in all your classes

➢ Becoming class president

➢ Becoming Student Council President

➢ Becoming Homecoming King or Queen

➢ Becoming prom King or Queen

➢ Making the football, track, swimming, or bowling team, etc.

➢ Graduating at the top of your class

➢ Being accepted into a graduate program

➢ Receiving a full scholarship to the school of your choice

"Success consists of getting up just one more time than you fall."

– Oliver Goldsmith

A non-realistic goal is to become the principal of your school or the president of your college while you're still a student in school. You get the point, right? There are no limits to your goals, just make sure they're realistic.

Timely

Last but not least, your goals must be timely. What good is having a goal if you never assign a time frame to accomplish it? A great way to achieve this is to put your goals into one of three categories.

The categories are long-term goals, intermediate goals, and short-term goals.

Long-term goals can range from 2-5 years. These are goals that you set based on where you see yourself within that time. Your goal may be to attend a college or university. You may have a goal to secure an internship at a highly reputable company or firm. Your goal may be to become the valedictorian of your graduating class. Make sure you take the time to figure out the big picture (long-term goal).

Intermediate or mid-range goals are 1-2 years in length. For example, if you are a freshman, one of your mid-range goals could be to join a club or organization so that you can meet new people. Mid-range goals also allow you to assess the halfway mark of your long-term goals.

Short-term goals are those that can be achieved within a year or less.

Note: try to make sure all three categories of your goals complement each other.

"My success just evolved from working hard at the business at hand each day."

– Johnny Carson

An important ingredient to goal setting and goal achievement is daily action. If you take action every day, working towards your goals, you will achieve them. As an author and leadership speaker, I also take a daily approach towards accomplishing my goals. For instance, one of my goals is to become a world-renowned motivational speaker and consultant, impacting millions of lives. To accomplish this grand goal, I follow a daily and weekly regimen. Here is a sample of my daily regimen.

- Read for personal development
- Listen to motivational podcasts
- Practice speeches
- Practice quotes
- Research target market areas
- Learn new vocabulary words; new ways of expression
- Review footage from previous presentations, reflection, and self-evaluation

"I've failed over and over and over again in my life, and that is why I succeed."

– Michael Jordan

What can you do as part of your daily regimen to accomplish your goals?

_____

_____

_____

_____

_____

_____

_____

_____

_____

_____

_____

_____

_____

_____

_____

_____

_____

_____

_____

_____

"I attribute my success to this – I never gave or took any excuse."

– Florence Nightingale

3

NEXT LEVEL POTENTIAL

Realizing your potential

One day, a researcher decided to conduct a study on the behavior of fleas. You know the little bugs that get on your pet dog or cat. He put about ten to fifteen fleas into a container, which was about five inches in height with a closed lid.

Immediately, the fleas began to jump, trying to escape from the sealed container. The first thing the researcher realized was that each time the fleas attempted to jump out of the container, they would hit their heads on the lid and fall. For three days, this process continued. The fleas repeatedly jumped up, hit their heads, and fell back down.

Next, the researcher decided to take his experiment to another level by removing the lid from the container while the fleas were still jumping. After removing the lid, the researcher noticed that the fleas were still jumping, but not enough to jump out. They were only jumping to the height or the level of the lid and consequently falling.

"The greatest waste in the world is the difference between what we are and what we could become."

- Ben Herbster

The researcher was shocked! Thinking that the fleas would jump out of the container after the lid was removed, but this certainly was not the case. This is where I will pause the story and give you a quick lesson on fleas. Adult fleas are about 1/16 to 1/8-inches long, are wingless, have three pairs of legs, and are flattened vertically. Fleas can jump vertically up to seven inches and horizontally, thirteen inches.

So, what was limiting their potential? Before I answer that question, let's get a clear understanding of what potential really is. Potential is defined as existing possibility or being capable of developing into actuality. I like to say that your potential is the possibility of what you can do, have, or become.

Now back to the story about fleas. According to the facts about fleas, they had the potential and capability of jumping seven inches high. This would have been high enough to escape from the container, but because of the conditioning process, they did not. Their potential was not being fully maximized because of the limitations that had been set upon them by the lid on the container.

Now, I know you are probably saying the lid, come on. The researcher discovered that each time the fleas hit their heads, they were being conditioned to fall back and not jump high enough to escape.

"Success seems to be connected with action. Successful people keep moving. They make mistakes, but they don't quit."

– Conrad Hilton

As a result of the conditioning process, their potential level decreased.

When the lid was removed, the fleas were already conditioned to think that there was no need to jump higher than 5 inches. The fleas thought that the lid was there, and jumping out of the container is impossible. These fleas were conditioned to be limited by the lid.

What lid of limitation are you hitting your head on?

By now, you can see that these fleas all had potential that was not being fully utilized. Not to compare you to a flea, but you too have potential. Potential as a student, organization leader, business professional, dreamer, visionary, and much much more. You have the potential to excel in all of your classes and to get the best grades possible. The potential of becoming a student leader. The potential to go from being a mediocre leader to becoming a magnificent leader. The potential to go from good to great.

Maximizing your student potential

Now that you know that you have the potential to be more, have more, and do more, you must focus on maximizing your potential so that it is not misused or under-utilized. Take cell phones, for instance. The newer model cell phones can download music, movies, pictures, and not to mentioned connect to the internet.

"No one succeeds without effort… Those who succeed owe their success to perseverance."

– Ramana Maharshi

However, there are thousands of individuals who have these phones and only use them to make phone calls, send text messages, and take pictures. Now, I'm not saying that they are misusing their phones because they're not. What I am saying is that they are not using their phones to their full potential.

Are you using your full potential? If the answer is yes, remember that you can always better your best. Meaning, you can always reach the next level even if you feel like you have reached a high level. On the other hand, if you feel that you are not fully maximizing your potential you are not alone. Many students are not maximizing their potential. Fortunately, the great news is that you can.

How? Let's go back to the story about the fleas. At this point, the researcher decided to continue the experiment. The researcher introduced a new flea into the container that has not been conditioned by the lid of limitations, and immediately, that flea jumped out of the container. When the newly introduced flea jumped out, what do you think the others did? If you said they followed, you are absolutely correct. They realized that they were no different from the new flea, and if it jumped out, they could do the same.

"Success is a state of mind. If you want success, start thinking of yourself as a success."

– Joyce Brothers

One of my goals for writing this book is to let you, the person reading this book, at this moment, know that you can do anything you put your mind to. However, keep in mind that whatever you want to do will take work. The only time you will find success before work is in the dictionary. I recommend that if you want better grades, work towards that goal by studying more, asking more questions, getting a tutor, or forming a study group. Similar to the new flea helping the others, I'm here to help you jump out of your container. My friend, you have the potential to be a world changer.

Use the space below to write all of the areas in your life in which you feel you are not fully maximizing your potential.

Example: (Academically)

I always get a C on my math test.

_____

_____

_____

_____

_____

_____

_____

_____

"When it comes to success, there are no shortcuts."

– Bo Bennett

Now write how you will maximize your potential.

Example: I will ask my math instructor questions about the assignments I don't understand. I will sit at the front of the class, so I'm not distracted. I will spend more time studying first before hanging out with friends.

_____

_____

_____

_____

_____

_____

_____

Be a Leader not a follower

Peer Pressure: Good or Bad?

As you're walking down the halls headed to your economics class with your friends, you hear someone say, "Hey, let's skip class and go grab lunch." Everyone pauses for a moment and then reply, "Yeah. Let's go get lunch, forget economics." At this moment, you are faced with a challenge. Should you do the right thing and go to class? Or should you go to lunch and fit in with the others, so you don't look like the oddball?

"They succeed, because they think they can."

– Virgil

Look. If you go to class, you will feel good because you know you've made a morally correct decision. Some students choose to follow the crowd and do the morally incorrect things. Now, you may be asking yourself why someone would do something morally wrong. It's because of negative peer pressure and the outcome.

Peer pressure is when your classmates or people who are your age — your peers, try to influence how you conduct yourself or to get you to act on something. Here's another example. Let's say that your best friend is trying to influence you to fill out a college application or job application. He or she would pressure you to find all the requirements and criteria needed to attend that particular college or to get that job/internship. So, can peer pressure be good and bad?

Peer pressure can be either good or bad (positive or negative). Below are lists of the two types of peer pressure.

Positive peer pressure

Being encouraged to...

Study more, Join productive clubs and organizations, Read more, Eat healthier, Attend class on time, Avoid trouble, Stay focused, Stay positive, Meet friendly people, Attend a college or University

"Success is a journey, not a destination."

– Ben Sweetland

Negative Peer Pressure

Being pressured into...

Drinking, Smoking, Cutting or skipping class, Cheating on a test, Stealing, Having sex before you're ready, Fighting, Talking bad about others, Hanging out instead of studying, Lying.

Student Leadership

Employers today are looking for employees who are leaders and display excellent leadership abilities. One of the best ways to develop these skills is to practice using them while in school.

Some of the most important skills are: **Organization, Computer and Communication skills**

Organizational Skills

Are you organized? How effective are you at multitasking? Being well-organized and having the ability to multi-task are essential qualities of a student leader. I recommend that you use your phone, tablet, or computer to list your class assignments, tests, and projects. Another way to get organized is to use different color folders, as well as highlighters for each of your classes. Following these simple recommendations will help you to become more organized, pushing you to succeed.

"The road to success is always under construction."

– Lily Tomlin

Computer Skills

Are you afraid of computers? Some people are, but don't let that be you. Acquiring computer skills is essential to your future and success. Almost everywhere you look, there is a computer. Knowing how to operate a computer and basic software such as Word, Excel, and PowerPoint could be a skill that will give you an advantage over the next candidate interviewing for the same position.

Communication Skills

Communication skills will be fundamental while in school, the workforce, and life in general. Knowing how to read, write, and speak efficiently is necessary if you are interested in any of the following:

- **Joining clubs and organizations**

- **Applying for college**

- **Applying for scholarships**

- **Filling out job applications**

- **Signing a contract to play professional sports such as football, baseball, basketball, etc.**

- **Buying a home**

- **Buying a car**

- **Investing your money**

"Enjoy your sweat because hard work doesn't guarantee success, but without it, you don't have a chance."

– Alex Rodriguez

The sooner you develop your communication skills, the more prepared you'll be for these exciting experiences.

The Ultimate Student

U- Undeniable

Webster's Dictionary defines undeniable as indisputable, incapable of being denied. When you are on the path to Next Level Student Success, you must refuse to be hindered by setbacks or obstacles. You can have anything you want in life, but you will have to fight for it. *Steve Duncanson said it best, "Life is a fight for territory; when you stop fighting for what you want, what you don't want will automatically take over."*

While in pursuit of your dreams and goals, you must fight until those dreams and goals are achieved. One way to explain undeniable is to look at weeds in a garden. Whenever you hear analogies about weeds, they are usually in a negative way. But, let's positively examine weeds.

"Success is the sum of small efforts repeated day in and day out."

– Robert Collier

One thing about weeds are, no matter how many times you pull them out, cut them down, or spray poison on them, they will always grow back. When you are going after your dreams and goals, life will try to pull you out, cut you down, or spray poison on you (fear, doubt, shame, your past), but you must be just like those weeds and come back each time. You must be **Undeniable!**

L- Leadership of your life

A Leader is one in charge. Successful people take charge of their lives. There are two main things I feel someone exercising leadership over their life must do. They must be a <u>goal setter</u> and <u>action taker</u>. Why is goal setting so important? Well, your goals will serve as a road map on your journey throughout school and beyond. Then you must act to get the opportunities and pursue them. Remember, success is a journey, not a destination.

Once you set your goals, the next step is to take the necessary action. Have you ever met someone who talked about doing this and doing that, and they had all the plans, but they never took action? Is this person you? This reminds me of the three cats sitting on the fence.

If three cats are sitting on a fence, and two decides to jump off, how many cats are still sitting on the fence?

"The starting point of all achievement is desire."

– Napoleon Hill

When I first heard this, I thought only one cat remained, but then I realized that the two cats only decided to jump off the fence; however, they never took action. In the lives of most, action is the missing ingredient to their success. "Lights, Camera, **Action**!"

What's stopping students from living their dreams or achieving more? The number one deterrent is fear. A lot of people allow the fear of failure to prevent them from living their dreams or taking action on a particular goal.

You will never reach your goals or go to the next level if you don't take action. If you fail while in pursuit of a goal or dream, this does not mean that you are a failure. It just means you need to re-evaluate the steps that were taken and try again.

T-Tenacious

A person who is obstinate or persistent has tenacity. Whenever you are in the process of achieving greatness, the storms of life will show up. Storms may come disguised as academic, relational, financial, health, or even family problems. When the different storms, trials, and tribulations arise, you must have the tenacity to go through the storms to meet your dreams on the other side.

"I believe success is preparation because the opportunity is going to knock on your door sooner or later, but are you prepared to answer that?"

– Omar Epps

Willard Marriott, the founder of the Marriott Hotels, said, "Good timber does not grow with ease. The stronger the wind, the stronger the trees." I remember when I was driving from Miami, Florida to Ft. Myers, Florida, to give a presentation at Florida Gulf Coast University. Halfway through this two-hour drive, I was caught in a thunderstorm.

At that moment, I had two choices: pull over to the side of the road and wait out the storm out or drive through it. I decided to drive through the storm. Within a couple of minutes, the sun was shining again. The different storms, trials, and tribulations of life will come and try to steal, kill, destroy your dreams, and derail you from accomplishing your goals.

Whenever you hit a storm in your life, slow down and turn your headlights on (focus), then put both hands on the steering wheel and go through the storm. *"Be not afraid of going slowly; be afraid only of standing still" – Chinese proverb.*

Choose to be tenacious!

"The path to success is to take massive, determined action."

– Tony Robbins

I-Invest in yourself

"You will be the same person in five years that you are today, except for the people you meet, books you read, and audios you listen to."

-Charlie Tremendous Jones

Many people invest a lot of time, money, and energy on their physical appearance in the form of expensive clothes, jewelry, cosmetics, and fragrances, but still fail to shift the way they think.

To go to the next level, it is vital that you invest in developing your mind. A great way that you can do this is to surround yourself with positive people. Like it is said, *"association breeds assimilation."* While on your journey to becoming magnificent, you should network with individuals with who you share the same ambitions. Doing this is important as the more you are around positive energy, the more likely it is to become a part of your life.

Think of it this way, if you want to catch a cold, hang around people with colds. On the other hand, networking and associating with positive, purpose-driven individuals who want more out of life will motivate you to learn more, have more, and become more.

Dr. Dennis Kimbro said, "If you are the smartest person in your group, you need a new group."

It is said that a goose can fly 75% farther with other geese, than alone. Just like these geese, you too should be in formation.

"The key to success is action, and the essential in action is perseverance."

– Sun Yat-sen

One Clydesdale horse can pull a 2000-pound wagon alone. Two Clydesdales harnessed together, moving together on the same path can pull 20,000 pounds, which is ten times more. The lesson is to connect with positive, goal-oriented, purpose-driven people. Another great way to invest in yourself is to read positive books and listen to positive audios like podcasts or YouTube clips.

Mark Twain said, "The man who does not read good books has no advantage over the man who cannot read them." Why should one invest in themselves through positive books and audios? Well, according to studies by psychologists, 87% of the average person's self-talk is negative. Daily a person thinks 40,000 to 50,000 thoughts. Of those, 34,000-43,500 are negative in nature. Constantly reading and listening to positive material helps to dilute much of the negative thoughts programmed in our subconscious mind since birth. Some enriching positive books and audios will provide this reinforcement.

Remember this:

What you think, determines what you say.

What you say, determines what you do.

What you do, determines your habits.

Your habits, determine your destiny.

Make the investment in yourself!

"The key to success is to keep growing in all areas of life – mental, emotional, spiritual, as well as physical."

– Julius Erving

M- Motive

What is motive? Webster defines motive as something that causes a person to act in a certain way or to do a certain thing. What is your motive? If you want to go to the next level, it's important that you define your "why."

"Your Why" will serve as the fuel to your engine, propelling you in the direction of your dreams and goals. I recommend that you write your reason/why down on a 3x5 notecard, carry it with you or type it in the notes section in your phone and review it daily.

Example: Eat healthier and get enough sleep at night– to perform at your highest level all the time.

My reason for becoming a professional speaker, author, and coach was so I could positively impact the world while being able to provide for my family and others in a significant way. You must define your why!

"Before everything else, getting ready is the secret of success."

– Henry Ford

A- Attitude Awareness

"Your attitude will determine your altitude."

Attitude is defined as the posture or bearing of a person, a state of mind. While on your journey, always strive to maintain a positive attitude. This is pivotal to your success. The process might be longer or slightly different than what you had in mind. Still, a positive attitude will give you clarity of thought to make quality changes (if needed).

T-Teachable

Can your mind be retrained? I believe that a great way to go from here to there is to be mentored or coached by someone successful in your field. Having a mentor or tutor will cut your learning curve by at least 50%.

You will be learning from the many mistakes made by your mentor, as well as all the years of experience your mentor has gained. Utilizing a mentor, tutor or coach is like having a fresh pair of eyes looking at you to help correct any flaws you may have. Many may say that Michael Jordan, Lebron James, or even Kobe Bryant are among some of the world's best basketball players to have ever played the game. What most people don't realize is that even these guys, as great as they are, had a mentor or coach. Consider getting a mentor or coach to help you reach the next level in your life.

"I believe any success in life is made by going into an area with a blind, furious optimism."

– Sylvester Stallone

E-Excitement and Expectation

The last tip in this formula is always to stay excited and always have a spirit of expectation. When I'm speaking to an audience, I always tell them to get excited and stay excited because things happen when you're excited. When you are excited, you begin to attract all the resources and people into your life who will assist you in accomplishing your dreams and goals.

Examples:

I expect...   To be healthy

To be happy

To be employed

To own a business

To have a loving family

To be financially secure

To have a nice home

To drive a nice car

To impact millions of lives

To have a positive attitude

To have an **Ultimate Day**

"The secret of our success is that we never, never give up."

– Wilma Mankiller

Feel free to review this chapter over and over until these tips become an everyday habit. Once you implement these eight tips into your life, you will, without a doubt, add value to your life, which would increase your chances of success.

So, remember while on your journey to success, be undeniable, take leadership of your life, be tenacious, invest in yourself, define your motive(s), be aware of your attitude, be teachable, stay excited, and expect great things to happen in your life.

Notes, Visions and Ideas

_____

_____

_____

_____

_____

_____

_____

_____

_____

_____

"The person without a purpose is like a ship without a rudder."

—Thomas Carlyle

4

NEXT LEVEL PURPOSE

It's extremely important that everything you do; you do with a purpose in mind. I have watched so many students struggle with certain situations because they were not operating with a purpose. They aimlessly got involved and seemingly got nowhere. When you have and operate with purpose, you always have a destination. Meaning purpose gives you something to aim for.

Running outside versus running on a treadmill

Do you think that there's a difference between running outside and running on a treadmill? Other than one is inside and the other one outside? Well, after engaging in both, I have found one major difference that most individuals overlook. When you exercise indoors on a treadmill, you are actually running in place, getting absolutely nowhere. On the other hand, when you run outside, you always have a destination, even if you run from your home to the mailbox or the end of the street, you still reach a destination. In both of these examples, the activity is the same, but the physical results are vastly different.

My friend, having a purpose is exactly the same. It gives you a sense of direction and destination to shoot for.

"Success is nothing more than a few simple disciplines, practiced every day."

– Jim Rohn

Identify and pursue

Have you taken the time to stop and identify <u>why</u> you do what you do? It's very important that you stop, take a moment, breathe, and clearly identify the people, places, and things you are involved with. Sometimes, we have to slow down to speed up. Meaning, allocating time to see if what we're engaged in is helping or hurting us. Identifying does just that. Purpose helps save time, energy, and, in some cases, money because once again, it gives you a sense of direction.

Take a few minutes to identify what you do and also why you do it. I want you to jot down every activity, organization, club, and any other actions with which you are involved.

What

(Clubs, organizations, classes, etc)

Why

(The reason for engaging)

_____   _____

_____   _____

_____   _____

_____   _____

_____   _____

_____   _____

"There is simply no substitute for hard work when it comes to achieving success."

– Heather Bresch

After closely identifying all of your what's, I now want you to analyze your why's. They should be in alignment with the outcomes that you desire. If they are not, I highly advise that you re-evaluate the activities that you are a part of.

Know that you know

Have you ever known anyone who attended a particular school just because their friends went there? Or because it's the largest and most popular school in the district or state? Maybe because they seemingly have the best athletic programs, or perhaps, the best-looking girls or guys. Or for the simple reason that it's close to their home.

Believe it or not, these are just a few reasons why students attend certain schools. My question to you after everything mentioned above would be, what purpose does it serve? Is the decision going to better you as a person/student? Is it going to help you in your future endeavors, such as college or your career? Think about that. Now, I'm not suggesting that the reasons mentioned above are not valid. In fact, some may very well be parallel to your purpose.

"The most important single ingredient in the formula of success is knowing how to get along with people."

– Theodore Roosevelt

For instance, if you have a strong passion for sports and believe that your life's purpose is sports-centered, it might be a great idea to attend a school that thrives on excellent athletic programs. It's all about figuring out what will benefit you the most. Know that whatever decisions you make now are going to benefit you in the future.

A Success Story

Let me give you some examples. The school that I attended had different academies to choose from, similar to majors in college. Meaning, I had a choice of what program of study I wanted to pursue. Programs such as Residential Construction, Drafting, Health, Industry Technology, Fanny Mae (Finance), Diesel Mechanics, and many more were available.

These options allowed students to learn or enhance their knowledge and skills for their future goals. Many students that already had an idea of what they wanted to pursue enrolled in an academy that complemented their desired outcome. In other words, most students enrolled in specific programs with a purpose in mind. This gave a sense of direction, and ultimately, the ability to save time, energy, and money.

"Success is not the key to happiness. Happiness is the key to success. If you love what you are doing, you will be successful."

– Albert Schweitzer

While in high school, I had a classmate who had dreams of becoming a doctor. He enrolled in the health academy because he realized that this particular area would assist him in becoming a doctor. Throughout his time in the health academy, he had the opportunity to learn the ins and outs of the health field. Furthermore, he also was able to volunteer at hospitals, practice what he learned on dummies, get internships, and much more. Today, he is living his dream. He is a Doctor at a prestigious hospital.

What's the point? The point is that the health academy helped him with direction as it related to his plans. It saved him from wandering from one field of study to another, and it gave him insight into what it takes to get to where he wanted to go.

Though your school might not have academies, there are still certain resources that will aid you down the path you desire. I suggest that you align yourself with clubs, organizations, courses, other outside activities, etc., that validate where you want to go. Please do not get caught up in activities that are not adding value to the outcome you desire.

"Success does not consist in never making mistakes but in never making the same one a second time."

– George Bernard Shaw

Bonus

College Bound

Although going to college does not automatically guarantee success, I highly recommend that you attend a university, college, trade, or vocational school. It is imperative that you engage in some post-secondary education after high school. Many students ask me about college, and I give it to them straight. "<u>No!</u>" I would say, "<u>attending college or even graduating from college does not automatically guarantee you success</u>." Success depends on applying what you have learned while in college.

Align yourself

As mentioned earlier, it's vital to align yourself with the major or course work that adds value to what you are looking to become. Make sure that it is something that interests you and not others. Remember, you only have one life to live, live it to satisfy the gifts, talents, and abilities given to you. I always tell college students or potential college attendees to align their future profession with their inner purpose and passion. In other words, to ensure that their passion/purpose is parallel with the major or career path that they select.

"Put your heart, mind, and soul into even your smallest acts. This is the secret of success."

– Swami Sivananda

I met a bright student who was very much into music. He had enough talent that he felt that he could make a career of it. However, many people around him always stressed the fact that he should attend college. The problem was this: the individuals in his life wanted him to attend college and major in studies that did not benefit his real genuine desire, which was music.

I often meet students that ask if I could give them some advice. They always express what they are interested in and how talented they are in a particular area. Then they always ask, "what should I do?" My reply is always very simple. Do it! If you plan to go to a four-year university, major in something that is going to help you with your interest. If it's not offered at your school or university, while in school, join clubs or groups involving your interest. For example, it would be beneficial for someone pursuing a music career to major in business or marketing, simply because you are going to have to know how to run, manage, and market yourself. Furthermore, it would make no sense at all for him to major in engineering with aspirations of pursuing a music career.

"Success isn't always about greatness. It's about consistency. Consistent hard work leads to success. Greatness will come."

– Dwayne Johnson

Specific knowledge versus General knowledge

I have a very simple philosophy as it relates to post-secondary education —Gain what I call specific knowledge instead of general knowledge. By investing in specific knowledge, you will save some of the unnecessary steps to getting to where you want to go.

General knowledge is good, but specific knowledge is great. General knowledge is obtaining a wide variety of information, which is much better than having no knowledge at all. However, specific knowledge is obtaining exactly what it takes to succeed in your chosen field. To be clear, I'm not suggesting that there is a cookie-cutter path towards what you want to achieve in the future. However, I am saying that the more specific you are in your studies, the closer you get to achieving a goal. For instance, my speaking and writing career has grown at a rapid pace due to the ability to learn from individuals who have achieved great things in my line of work. In other words, people who have already walked that path, been there and done that. People who are not afraid to show and mentor you on how to grow within a certain industry. I will talk about the power of mentorship in another chapter.

"Just remember, you can't climb the ladder of success with your hands in your pockets."

– Arnold Schwarzenegger

In order to really grow either in school and beyond, you have to pair with someone or something that can show you the ropes and give you *specifically* what you need. My mentors have done precisely that.

Because they had such tremendous success, over the past 15 years from motivational speaking and authoring books, they can now give that information and knowledge to others. Now the path is clearer and seems straighter. When you obtain general knowledge, it seems to cloud your mind because you are often clueless about what to do with it.

When I graduated with my Bachelor's degree in Business Administration, I was clueless on how to apply the information. I learned a lot. I mean, I learned so much information about business that it literally made my head spin! However, the information wasn't that valuable until I was able to apply it.

Now that I am an entrepreneur, I have learned to turn to others who can help me in my industry. I am now able to utilize *specific business tactics, techniques, strategies, information, and knowledge* from my mentor, who is assisting me in becoming the motivational speaker and author that I wish to be.

Remember, general knowledge is good, but specific knowledge is Great.

We should never stop learning,

earning or yearning.

\- Chris Morley

5

NEXT LEVEL STUDENT

Being a perpetual student is one of the cornerstones for Next Level Student Success and beyond. Many students fail to understand that being a student is much more than just learning in the classroom. A student is one who closely examines or investigates. The only way to truly grow and expand is to examine everything around you closely, including your dreams and your vision, as I discussed in chapter 1. This includes extra curriculum activities, such as clubs and organizations that you want to lead or be a part of. Basically, continuing to learn will expand your capacity and increase your chances of succeeding in your chosen endeavor.

The hardest thing to study

Have you ever wondered what the hardest thing to study was? I think I have truly figured it out. My friend, the hardest thing to study is yourself. Why? Often times we are not aware of the areas of our lives that we need to focus and work on. Someone once said that it's hard to see the picture when you are the frame. Meaning, sometimes it's difficult to see gifts, talents, and abilities when you are the one who possesses them.

"It's how you deal with failure that determines how you achieve success."

– Charlotte Whitton

I want you to become conscious of you. Know what your strengths and weakness are.

How do you focus on something you have no idea is lacking in your academic, social, or personal life? Identify your strengths and continue to work on them so that they can get even stronger. Likewise, identify your weaknesses and strive to improve those areas of your life. For example, if you recognize that you are having a difficult time studying, maybe you need to discover how you learn.

Discover how you learn best

It's imperative that you discover how you learn. Most students are clueless when it comes to how they learn, and the best way to study. I'm so excited about sharing this information with you because I had no clue about this information while I was a student.

There are three types of learning styles — seeing, hearing, and experiencing. Do you know which category fits you best? They are all vastly different as it relates to your ability to learn to your highest capacity.

"Success is getting what you want. Happiness is wanting what you get."

– Dale Carnegie

Learning by seeing

Learning by seeing is the element of visualizing information. These students learn best by seeing the information taught. In other words, they learn best with visuals such as graphs, charts, pictures, diagrams, illustrations, examples, etc. Learning by seeing is essential for students who thrive on memory and the power of visualization. This style is so effective because it allows you to backtrack mentally and visualize the information or concepts presented.

Learning by hearing

This style of learning is tied to students who are effective listeners. The capacity to learn for these students lies in the ability to receive information through hearing successfully. These students learn best from talking through or having someone explain the information presented. This style of learning allows for information transfer into the conscious and ultimately subconscious mind of a person. When you need the information, perhaps, for a test, experiment, etc., you will hear in your mind what you have been depositing into it.

"There are no secrets to success. It is the result of preparation, hard work, and learning from failure."

– Colin Powell

Learning by experiencing

Learning by experience is probably the most common or effective way of learning, as it utilizes the other two factors of learning— learning by seeing and learning by hearing.

Learning by experiencing is, in most cases, the most effective way of learning because it involves hands-on activity. These students learn best from actually engaging and doing what is presented to them.

Based on what you just read, which category do you fall into? Understand that we all learn with all three styles, but which do you utilize the most? Once you have identified your style, use it. Put it to use. Make it work for you, and I promise that you will be a better student and person.

Learn, learn and learn some more

Learn, learn, and learn some more! That's the name of the game. You can never learn too much. In fact, the more you learn, the more you realize and discover how much more there is to learn. I have found that the more you go, the more you grow. This means that the more you pursue something, the more you realize how deep or how much is tied to the pursuit.

"The secret of your success is determined by your daily agenda."

– John C. Maxwell

For instance, have you ever begun to study a specific topic within a subject, but when you started studying, you found other elements tied to that topic? That is because there is always information linked to other information.

Note: when you begin to study for a class or exam, never just jump right into a specific topic in your textbook. Read and muse over the information presented before and after the specific topic you are looking to study.

An example of this would be: skipping to the index to locate the page of a term or word, then going to that page and just reading the definition. Yes, you probably got the definition, but did you fully understand the meaning of that term? To really get the meaning and understanding of something, it is vital that you study the material before and after the core information. I guarantee this will give you a full understanding of whatever it is that you are looking up. This is precisely what learn, learn, and learn some more means. Most students/people settle for the sizzle when they could have the steak. Meaning, most never go deeper than the first and initial level of learning. Don't let that be you. Remember, the more you know, the more you grow.

"The secret of success is learning how to use pain and pleasure instead of having pain and pleasure use you. If you do that, you're in control of your life. If you don't, life controls you."

– Tony Robbins

Ask, ask, and ask some more

It is extremely important that you ask questions throughout your journey as a student and beyond. Better yet, ask for what you want. Ask your teachers, counselors, professors, and any other person who is willing to steer you down the right path. **There is no such thing as a dumb or stupid question.** Find someone who you connect with and ask, ask, ask.

Ask questions pertaining to the major you plan to pursue in college, and about career choices after college. Ask questions about what it takes to get to where you want to go. Ask questions about how they were able to transcend to where they are. Ask questions about what they feel you need to improve and ask about what they feel you are currently doing right. Ask about financial planning, setting goals both personally and professionally. Ask how to get better grades, how to study, and how to get an "A" in their class. Ask any question that surfaces in the forefront of your mind.

The term "ask" literally means to put a question to or to inquire after. It is important that you inquire after what it is that you are striving to achieve. Questioning opens up opportunities that you probably never thought would come your way.

"Your positive action, combined with positive thinking, results in success."

– Shiv Khera

Why people don't ask

Most students fail to ask for what they want because they fear the response. The bottom line is that most are afraid of hearing the word **NO**. This two-letter word to most is like the bogeyman of our vocabulary. The word **NO** has crippled and paralyzed several students to the point that it causes the inability to reach their full potential.

My friend, please do not be afraid to ask because the word **NO** has never hurt anyone. In fact, if someone tells you **NO**, that is an indication that maybe he or she is not supposed to occupy your space. Another reason why people do not ask is because of the fear of rejection. Have you ever been so terrified to engage in something new due to the fear of rejection? Maybe something that was so far out of your comfort zone, that you felt there was a possibility of rejection.

I can recall on numerous occasions when this happened to me, I was terrified! However, once I got moving and began performing the task at hand, the feeling of rejection lessened vastly. I want you to do the same. Step out and step up into the face of what seems to be a rejection. You will then find these situations are there to build character and make you stronger.

"A strong, positive self-image is the best possible preparation for success."

– Joyce Brothers

Ask and you shall receive!

I recall seeing homeless people asking for money when I worked in downtown Miami. One day as I was in my car, I noticed a guy asking for money under one of the bridges. He had a sign that read: **Homeless! Please spare change. God Bless you.** Other homeless people were sitting about 200ft from the first guy who did not have a sign at all. While waiting for the red light to change, I watched people give money to the man with the sign and not give to the others who did not have a sign.

The point is quite simple. **If you ask, you shall receive.** So I encourage you to ask for what you want while in school, and especially beyond. Ask for extra credit assignments, letters of recommendation, advice on selecting career options, a college (major), counseling, study buddies, tutoring, mentorship, notes, and any others that you can think of. **Ask!**

"Eighty percent of life's satisfaction comes from meaningful relationships."

-Brian Tracy

6

NEXT LEVEL RELATIONSHIPS

As you go through your school experience, remember to build positive relationships with everyone. I can't express this point enough. The relationships you develop will be of great benefit to you in the future. It's important that while at school, you start this process with your peers, teachers, administrators, principals, professors, etc.

Developing relationships with your teachers and professors can play a huge role when it comes down to getting letters of recommendation for a college application or a reference on an employment or internship application. Now you are probably saying that in five to ten years you will be established and you don't really need the help of your peers, teachers, and staff at your school. I would simply say stay open to the idea that you have developed positive relationships, and if you need help, it is potentially there for you.

"Some people dream of success, while other people get up every morning and make it happen."

– Wayne Huizenga

When I graduated from High School, I had no idea years after I graduated from college that I would be calling on teachers, counselors, and administrators for their help and support. In 2005, I decided that I wanted to make a transition from my profession to become a leadership and student success speaker, impacting the lives of young people positively.

Once I had that goal in mind, I immediately contacted my old high school and asked if I could come in to speak to students. Luckily, when I was in high school, I had wonderful relationships with my teachers, peers, and staff. Since then, I have gone back to the school and spoken to individual classes as well as the entire student body.

The point I'm trying to make is to work on developing positive and lasting relationships daily with your peers, teachers, and the staff members at your high school and college. One day, these relationships will be of great benefit to you and them.

"You Are The Average Of The Five People You Spend The Most Time With."

— Jim Rohn

7

NEXT LEVEL FRIENDS

This chapter is designed to guide you in defining and identifying the individuals who serve as assets to your success; people who don't want to pull you down, but rather lift you. One of my mentors, Delatorro McNeal, says that people are just like elevators; they can take you up or they can take you down. These individuals are students who are going in the same direction and traveling down the same path as you. My goal is to get you to understand that who you hang out with says who you are.

Let me break down what I mean. If I had only 30 minutes to spend with someone you associate with, I could tell you what type of person you are or will become without even meeting you. "See birds of a feather flock together." This simply implies that individuals who are similar to each other often spend time together.

What kind of bird are you? Are you the type of bird who needs a plethora of other birds to fly with? Or are you an **eagle** who needs little to no help soaring high through the sky?

"Some of the best lessons we ever learn are learned from past mistakes. The error of the past is the wisdom and success of the future."

– Dale Turner

My friend, I want you to become an eagle, one who relies on its own with the determination to succeed. Often, especially in grade school, students think that the more people flock around them, the cooler they are.

Please understand that I'm not saying that you should disassociate yourself from anyone. No, that's insane. I am suggesting that you be selective in whom you let into your space. One of the most effective ways to do this is to ask yourself some questions. A guy by the name of Anthony Robbins said something you can take into consideration. He said that the quality of our lives is determined by the quality of questions that we ask ourselves. Sounds good to me, what about you?

On the next page, I want to ask you some questions. Following the questions, I want you to think and insert a name that best answers the question. Ready! Let's go!

"Give me six hours to chop down a tree, and I will spend the first four sharpening the ax."

—Abraham Lincoln

Questions to consider

1) Who do you share your deepest thoughts and feelings with?

_____

_____

2) Who celebrates your successes?

_____

_____

3) What friends/classmates has the same mindset that you portray?

_____

_____

4) Who keeps you focused on your future?

_____

_____

5) Which student(s) stretches and encourage you to be a better person/student?

_____

_____

"Without continual growth and progress, such words as improvement, achievement, and success have no meaning."

– Benjamin Franklin

When you've answered these questions, you should have a better understanding of the individuals that you should associate with. If one of the names you came up with repeated more than once, that means that he or she should be the number one person who you let in your space. Also, if there is someone who did not appear on the list, then you may want to re-evaluate your flock.

Your income as a professional would be the average of the five people with whom you spend the most time with. If you're the smartest student in your group, guess what, you need another group. If you're the most intelligent student in your group, you need another group. Lastly, if you make the best grades in your group, guess what, you need another group! Your ultimate goal while in school as a student is to totally enmesh yourself with other students from whom you can learn and grow.

"Success is how high you bounce when you hit bottom."

– George S. Patton

The Process of Elimination

While on your journey as a student, you are going to encounter people who can either help or hurt you. **How will you choose?** As I reiterate and think about the various reality television shows that have struck the airways, it's amazing to understand the purpose of them. I mean, besides high ratings and fame, there is a deeper understanding and purpose of these shows.

Every show from "American Idol" to "The Bachelor," all had one basic premise. They all utilized *the process of elimination* to distinguish the person or group that would best fit what they are looking for. When you look beyond the drama and hype, there are messages behind the mess.

Making the Band with Sean "Diddy" Combs was one of my favorites while I was a college student because it connected with the essence of real life. For those of you who are not familiar with this show, let me explain. Making the Band was a show that was produced by the owner and CEO of Bad Boy Entertainment Sean Combs, also known as "Puffy," "P. Diddy" or "Diddy" depending on his mood.

"People should decide what success means for them, and not be distracted by accepting others' definitions of success."

– Tony Levin

Along with his team of experts, Diddy traveled to five to ten different cities searching for new talent that would ultimately become a part of a band and Diddy's record label. Here's what I want you to catch. Diddy was searching for <u>just</u> five new talented artists that would complement each other while in the band. The most amazing aspect of the show was this: Tens of thousands of artists tried out, but only five made it. It was fascinating to me to see how Diddy and his crew narrowed tens of thousands of artists down to <u>just</u> five.

Throughout the show, Diddy implemented challenges that allowed him to make the necessary cuts, which led him closer to the core group of five artists. With that said, I now want to challenge you to challenge the people/students around you. Notice that Diddy chose the artists who complemented each other. I want you to do the same thing. I suggest that you select about 3 to 5 people/students who complement you.

I know you're probably asking yourself what does that mean? I'm glad you asked. Complement in this sense means balance, match, harmonize, etc. My friend, you want to surround yourself with individuals with whom you can establish balance. Someone who's an excellent match for the direction in which you are headed.

"Success is where preparation and opportunity meet."

– Bobby Unser

Finding the right match

The right match will not come easily. Why? Because someone as unique as yourself demands the right to possess top quality people in your circle. I remember my days in high school, in my freshman year, I had about 60 students with whom I openly associated with. Back then, I did not know about protecting my space and who I let in it. However, over my next three years, through the process of elimination, I established a mastermind group.

A mastermind group is simply a cluster of individuals who assist each other in becoming the master at any chosen endeavor. My group consisted of four of my closest friends. Now, understand that these were not just people that I kept around because they were friends. I kept them because they added value to my life.

"Ambition is the path to success. Persistence is the vehicle you arrive in."

– Bill Bradley

Let me give you some indications to use to determine if someone or something is adding value to your life.

Someone who adds value to your life:

- **Keeps you away and out of trouble.**
- **Positively speaks about you and your life.**
- **Wants to see you succeed in any endeavor.**
- **Encourages you.**
- **Helps you grow as a student/person.**
- **Makes you feel better about yourself, situation, or issue after leaving their presence.**
- **Enhances your imagination.**
- **Increases your self-esteem, self-worth, and confidence.**
- **Stretches you, tell you the truth, and hold you accountable.**
- **Upholds and sets high standards.**
- **Is concerned about your well-being.**

These are just a few indicators of people who are adding value to your life. If someone that you associate with does not meet some of these indicators, it will behoove you to associate with someone who does.

"For success, attitude is equally as important as ability."

– Walter Scott

Friendships and relationships are similar to getting an appraisal on a home. When you own a home, the ultimate goal is to build equity so that the home accumulates value. Once the home accumulates value, it then begins to appreciate rather than depreciate. My friend, you want to build valuable relationships so that they will begin to appreciate and not depreciate. You do that by having high standards and stick to the indicators mentioned above.

The desperation of association

With all of the talk regarding you having people/students that complement you, don't be surprised if those individuals fail to show up immediately. After dealing with students and experiencing being a young adult, I have discovered that sometimes, students settle for mediocre relationships simply because they want someone around. Please don't let this be you.

I have come to know countless students or people who possessed tremendous potential and talent but allowed individuals to pull them away from achieving their goals. Have you ever known anyone who had terrific talents, gifts, and abilities but was drawn away by people who did not have their best interest at heart? I see it happen all the time, not just to students, but to people in general. Most of the time, the feeling of loneliness creeps in, and consequently, people end up living and achieving beneath their ability.

*"He has achieved success who has worked well,
laughed often, and loved much."*

– Elbert Hubbard

Three young men

I knew three young men that fit directly into this category. They had enormous amounts of talent but allowed negative associations to draw them away, and ultimately, squandered their gifts, talents, and abilities. The three young men whom I'm alluding to were all amazing high school football players. They were so talented that at the conclusion of their junior years, they were all awarded full scholarships to a major University. Man, were they excited —excited about the opportunity to play for the university and the possibility of being drafted into the National Football League.

Everything seemed great until they made some bad choices. Choices that caused all of them to lose their scholarships, and ultimately, end up in prison. Unfortunately, the reason they fell into this predicament is because of the people they associated with. They got into huge amounts of trouble simply because they hung around people who did not have their best interest at heart. These football players were meant to fly high.

You are meant to fly high, be aware of individuals who act as boulders tied to your kite, impeding it from reaching the altitude of success.

"Success is not in never failing, but rising every time you fall!"

– Jonathan Taylor Thomas

Association and Academics

As mentioned earlier in this chapter, you are who you associate with. Think about it. When you see a student-athlete, you normally see other student-athletes with them. When you see a drama student, typically, you would see other drama students. Likewise, when you see a member of the SGA, you most likely will see other members as well. And guess what? If you see one student who does well academically, most likely, you will see others that also do well academically.

The point is that there is no possible way that you can do well academically or professionally and associate with students who do not. Now that's not to imply that you cannot assist students who need help academically; in fact, that is a part of the growth process. If you desire to do well academically, I suggest that you surround yourself with others who are achieving what you want to accomplish. It's just that simple! Speaking from my experience, I recommend study clusters along with your willpower and determination to generate the best grades possible. Study clusters are groups that come together to study, but most importantly, to learn and grow from each other.

"If everyone is moving forward together, then success takes care of itself."

– Henry Ford

Associate with individuals who stretch you to be the best you that you can be; your study cluster members should always have an open mind to learning from each other. However, study clusters are only one of the many avenues to improve your academics, and will only take you so far. The willpower and determination to succeed is ultimately yours. No one can generate the grades for you; that's why it's up to you.

Notes, Visions and Ideas

_____

_____

_____

_____

_____

_____

_____

_____

_____

_____

"Many of life's failures are people who did not realize how close they were to success when they gave up."

– Thomas A. Edison

8

NEXT LEVEL PROMOTION

(Getting involved in Clubs, Organizations, and Community Service)

While in school, I recommend that you gain as much knowledge and leadership experience as possible. A great way to achieve this is to get involved in clubs and organizations. One of the first steps you can take is to get involved immediately. Begin by researching all of the clubs and organizations at your school to see what they offer. Furthermore, see how they can benefit you the most. Here are just a few clubs and organizations your school may have.

Student Government Association, Debate Team, Dance, Trio, FFA, FBLA, Fraternities, Sororities, Chess club, Drama club, Art club...and many more.

The purpose of this chapter is to get you to understand that the more visible you are, the better chances you have at success. Why? If you're visible, then people will know who you are. Imagine having the most talent, ability, and skills but not succeeding because the world doesn't know who you are.

"Every skill you acquire doubles your odds of success."

– Scott Adams

Believe it or not, this happens quite often. That's why it is vital that you display yourself and your abilities as much as possible. Think about it. There are plenty of people with so many skills and abilities, but go unnoticed because no one knows who they are. Please don't let this be you.

Now, if when researching school clubs and organizations, you fail to find one or a few that interest you, you can always start one. Find out how you would go about starting your own club or organization and begin the process right away. The process of starting a club will help you to develop and nurture leadership skills.

In finding a club or organization that's right for you, find one that aligns with your interests. Once you have found the right club(s) or organization(s) for you, make sure you do the following to ensure that there is a win/win situation for you and the club or organization.

Make sure that once you make a commitment to that club or organization, you honor it. How do you honor the commitment? Attend all meetings. Arrive on time and ready to learn. Contribute your time, energy, efforts, talents, and ideas. Focus on adding value and quality to that club and continue to raise the bar for the incoming members.

"Don't wait to be successful at some future point. Have a successful relationship with the present moment and be fully present in whatever you are doing. That is success."

– Eckhart Tolle

What clubs and organizations are you currently involved in?

_____

_____

_____

_____

_____

Are they aligned with your passion and interest?

Yes _____   No _____

Community Service

Don't Wait!

Don't Wait!

Don't Wait!

Don't wait to begin taking on your community service obligations. If community service is a part of your graduation requirements or mission of your club/organization, please do not procrastinate. Find out from your guidance counselor (if in grade school) or from student services how many hours of service are needed and get started.

"My powers are ordinary. Only my application brings me success."

– Isaac Newton

The earlier you start, the better position you will be in to accumulate as many hours as you can. The more community service hours you have will benefit you when it comes to applying for scholarships, colleges, universities, internships, and job applications after college. Make a list of all the places you would like to do community service, contact them, and begin.

Get Started Today!

Below, jot a list of potential community service projects that you can start today.

Community Service List:

1) _____

2) _____

3) _____

4) _____

5) _____

"One important key to success is self-confidence. An important key to self-confidence is preparation."

– Arthur Ashe

9

NEXT LEVEL

After closely examining and being a continuous student of successful people, I have found that one key ingredient is the willingness to go that extra mile. This involves pushing yourself beyond where the average person stops. Going beyond the crowd. Having a drive and passion for doing extra. One of my favorite books is The Magic is in the Extra Mile by Larry DiAngi. I highly recommend this book to anyone bound for success. Most people do enough just to get by. Do you know anyone like that?

Students who study just enough to pass a test with a "C," resist the effort of studying hard enough to receive an "A." Students who just do enough to pass the course, refuse to go the extra mile to do exceptionally well in the course. Students who are accepted into a club or organization, but fail to participate or give their input. Athletes, who make the team, but fail to work diligently on their craft.

Just making it is not enough. Going the extra mile, that is, doing things that are not expected of you will take you a long way. While doing that extra mile, you will find few people on the mile with you.

"We were all born with a certain degree of power. The key to success is discovering this innate power and using it daily to deal with whatever challenges come our way."

– Les Brown

However, you must stay focused and determined to make things happen.

Doing what is not expected of you will catch the attention of your professors, teachers, principals, counselors, peers, and others. This is a great way to get a teacher to remember you. That is if you are trying to build a relationship or to do exceptionally well in their class. Going the extra mile is a sign that you are a go-getter, and you are willing to do more than you must.

Dwayne Wade

My wife's favorite professional basketball player is Dwayne Wade, the retired Miami Heat Superstar. I can recall an interview after he won the NBA Finals M.V.P award. The reporter asked him how he was able to compete and play at such a high level throughout the playoffs. He replied by saying he made it this business to practice after practice. In other words, when all of his teammates went home after practice, he stayed behind to engage in additional workouts.

Wade mentioned that there were many nights where he would enter the gym all by himself. Now keep in mind that this is after a full day of practice with the entire team. However, Dwayne knew that if he wanted to get better, he had to work harder. This is a prime example of going that extra mile.

"The best revenge is massive success."

– Frank Sinatra

The late Kobe Bryant also lived by this same mentality. In fact, it was called the Mamba Mentality.

I shared this story to express the importance of going beyond the norm. Although the price to pay may be more, the rewards are also greater. I want you to get the mindset of "whatever it takes." If it takes you some additional studying to ace a test, then so be it. If it takes you two years to become the president of a desired organization, then so be it. Let yourself be free and open to the opportunity of going the extra mile.

Never be satisfied

When I was in high school, I had a teacher by the name of Ms. White-head. This woman was and still, to this day, an amazing leader, moti-vator, and most of all, exceptional teacher.

Ms. Whitehead is the kind of teacher who appears to intimidate students mainly because she forces you to learn with her teaching style and pushes students to their maximum capacity. She always stressed the importance of going the extra mile and doing more than what was expected. Ms. Whitehead instilled in her students, day in and day out, to never be satisfied.

"One secret of success in life is for a man to be ready for his opportunity when it comes."

– Benjamin Disraeli

"You might do some work that you feel proud of, however never be content with just that. There is much more to be accomplished."

Wow! What a teacher! There is much more for you to accomplish, so never ever be satisfied with where you are or what you have. Remember that the more you dig into something, the more will be revealed to you. So, I encourage you to dig deep into your studies.

Dig deep into your college courses. Dig deep into future goals and endeavors. Dig deep into the information that you seek and never be satisfied.

Don't wait to shine

This is a big one. Don't wait to shine is such an important attribute of school that can make or surely break you. What do you think I mean when I say, "don't wait to shine"? Take a few moments to jot exactly what comes to your mind when you hear this phrase.

_____

_____

_____

_____

_____

_____

_____

_____

"Success is doing ordinary things extraordinarily well."

– Jim Rohn

Don't wait to shine has everything to do with your grade point average (G.P.A). Now, this is not to say that you should wait to shine as a student leader because you should not. In fact, you should start right away, making your presence known from day one in a positive way. However, your grade point average should be a high priority on your list. I have known numerous students who felt that they had all the time in the world. They failed to give their studies and classes the attention that they needed and ended up trying to catch. In fact, this happened to me.

I literally did not buckle down and take my classes seriously until my junior year. All of a sudden, I realized that two years had passed, and I only had two years left. The most important thing to remember is that once your G.P.A is lower, it is extremely difficult to improve and bring it back up.

Basically, I had to strive to get straight A's so that I could raise my G.P.A to where I wanted it to be. **So, don't wait to shine.** Come out of the gates ready to do well academically. Many students believe that they have so much time. Do I have news for you! Time flies! Do not spend your time playing catch up, but spend your time trying to stay ahead.

"Fall seven times and stand up eight."

-- Japanese Proverb

10

NEXT LEVEL BELIEF

My friend, your power to succeed is based on your power to believe. Excellent grades, leading an organization or club, becoming an effective student leader, passing all test, and accomplishing all other aspects of school will never happen if you fail to believe in yourself and your abilities. Belief is really the one principle that must be activated and utilized to succeed in any area of your life, school included.

I've encountered many students who do not do well academically because they do not believe in themselves. This is not just present in grade school, but in college, and adulthood as well. Belief is the driving force behind your talents, skills, and ability to perform. Have you ever wondered why someone succeeded at something that you thought someone else was better at? I know there have been plenty of times when I wondered how in the world some individuals made it as far as they did.

"Never mind what others do; do better than yourself, beat your own record from day to day, and you are a success."

– William J. H. Boetcker

How did some singers and artists on the radio make it so far? How did some professional athletes make it to a certain level, when in popular opinion, others were apparently better? The answer is quite simple. These people had or have a greater belief system. It is impossible to go beyond what you believe. Belief gives you that deep inner knowing and insight that you need to take the next step.

Belief cures all

As I study and analyze students/people, I have come to the conclusion that belief transcends every tool that can be utilized to push you ahead. These include a high school diploma, a college degree, an excellent education, a great upbringing, a mentor, great friends, loving and caring parents, and any others that you can think of. See, all of these attributes mean absolutely nothing if you do not believe in YOU. I have come to know several students/people who have great credentials but lack the belief to utilize these credentials.

Do you know anyone like that? Someone you look at and say man, "you have two degrees, why are you not putting them to good use?" Or "man you can sing. Why not pursue a career in the music industry?" "Hey, you can cook. Why don't you pursue studies in culinary arts to become a chef?"

"When love and skill work together,
expect a masterpiece."

– John Ruskin

Now I'm not saying that this is always the reason, but for the most part, people do not pursue something due to the lack of belief in themselves. My friend, you need to know that you are the one.

Know that you know

Throughout high school and college, I knew that I would one day become successful. The funny thing is that I had no clue as to where my success would come from. However, day in and day out, I carried myself with a successful attitude, knowing that the day would come for me to step into my greatness. I think it's pretty evident that I have stepped into it because of the book you are holding right now. Throughout school and even beyond, you must walk with a swagger that says, "I know that I'm supposed to be successful."

Someone once said that long before you get something, you must first act as if you already possess it. This shows that you are cognizant of the greatness that lies on the inside of you.

"The most beautiful thing you can wear is confidence."

– Blake Lively

The one

From this point forward, I want you to start believing that you are the one. The one for what? The one for success. The one reaching for greatness. The one to earn excellent grades. The one to lead an organization. The first one to graduate from high school or college. The one to pursue your dreams. The one to graduate at the top of your class. The one to be the one.

Often, we disregard the fact of being the one because we are so focused on others being the one. Fortunately, I have news for you. You have just been tagged. You're it! You're the one! Do you believe it? I hope so because you have been designed and created to accomplish major things in life. Don't let anyone tell you anything different.

I want you to complete the sentence below.

I am the one to:

_____

I am the one to:

_____

I am the one to:

_____

"Believe in yourself! Have faith in your abilities!
Without a humble but reasonable confidence
in your own powers you cannot be
successful or happy."

– Norman Vincent Peale

Yes, you are the one, and it is more than possible for you to be the one to accomplish all that you have written.

From where does belief stem?

Belief stems from all sorts of places. From your past, your experiences, your thoughts, what you hear or have heard, what you say, how you were raised, your environment, the beliefs of your parents, your friends, what you see on television, and many others. These are all elements that shape your belief about who you are, what you stand for, and what you hold to be true.

Many students are hindered because of past experiences that have shaped their beliefs. For instance, have you ever failed a test and when it was time to retake the test, you had doubts about passing it? In other words, because of past failures, you develop the mindset of defeat for the next test. That's how belief is formed. Now, going into the new test, you already have a preconceived notion that there's a strong possibility that you may fail again.

I see this happen constantly. But guess what? It works both ways. What if you have experienced success on a particular exam or test. This test could be the SAT or ACT. Will you be more confident and possess the belief that you can score well again?

"You've got to put in the work. And you've got to play with confidence. You've got to believe in yourself."

– Paul Pierce

My guess would be yes. Why? Based on your past success with the exam, you are expecting to have future success on the next exam.

This is how belief shapes itself. And once again, it comes in many forms. Go back and review the elements mentioned in the first paragraph of this section. Keep in mind that we all have come across situations that we just did not believe we could overcome. So, I guess the next question would be: how do you break the cycle? How do you snap the process that is trying to establish itself in your life?

It's vital that you learn how to shift your thoughts of defeat to thoughts of victory. You do that by replacing every negative thought with a positive one. In other words, as soon as you get a negative thought or experience a negative situation, you have to instantly remove it and replace it with something that is going to keep you progressively moving in the right direction. First and foremost, you have to keep on shooting.

Regardless of previous outcomes, you have to keep pushing for the outcome that you want. Even if you failed a test five times, keep coming back. Along with the replacing method, your persistence will always pay off.

"Big Shots are only little shots who keep shooting!"

—Christopher Morley

Successful people keep coming back again and again and again until they achieve what they want. What about you? Will you keep on shooting? Remember, you can do it if only you believe.

Keep on shooting

"Big Shots are only little shots who keep shooting!"

—Christopher Morley

In grade school, college, work, relationships, and life in general, most people fail due to the lack of consistency. I heard a story about a basketball player who continuously worked on his jump shot. Day in and day out, he worked on his shot because he knew the more you work on something, the better you become.

One particular day while in the gym shooting around, he noticed that his shot wasn't falling. And for about a good 20 minutes, he struggled to make a few baskets in a row when normally he'd make consecutive shots. However, this day was different. The ball was just not going into the basket. Finally, after about 40 minutes, he was in the zone. Making shot after shot after shot. He later explained that most people give up and stop shooting when they start missing.

"Have confidence that if you have done a little thing well, you can do a bigger thing well too."

– David Storey

The only way to start making shots is to keep on shooting. Do not get discouraged when you "miss shots" because the more you miss, the closer you are to making one.

This is a vital success principle to adopt while in high school, college, and in your personal life as well. Whatever you want to achieve in life or in school, it is important that you continue to surge forward and shoot for it even when you have failed before. Failure doesn't exist when you learn something from it. Failure is the bridge to success. There are thousands of people who never reach their goals because they have given up and lost all hope. Don't let that be you.

Keep going until you get what you want! If you want better grades, keep studying and work hard to earn them. If you want to be the president of a specific club or organization, then keep working until you become the president. If you want to be an excellent student, do exceptionally well on the SAT or ACT examinations, pass every test, be looked upon as a student leader, improve your relationships, become more social, increase your chances of success, do whatever it takes to get there.

"Confidence is everything. Confidence is what makes that simple white tee and jeans look good."

– Ciara

Before I move any furthermore, I want you to write down a few things that you want to achieve. These can be educational or personal goals. What matters is that you have something written down.

_____

_____

_____

_____

_____

_____

_____

Set high expectations

When you begin to believe, you begin to set high expectations for yourself. Why? It's because you now see yourself in a different light. When you start to believe that you can do better academically, you then set higher expectations than you did before. When you believe that you can perform at the high school or college level, you then begin to set higher standards and expectations for yourself. Setting high expectations is so critical. My mentor says that in life, we do not get what we want, but in most cases, we get what we expect.

"My style has changed and evolved mainly because I've grown to have more confidence in myself."

– Kevin Durant

What are you expecting? It's imperative that we expect great things. However, keep in mind that your expectations are born out of what you believe. Many students never get to the level of setting high expectations because they fail to believe in themselves. Don't let that be you. Build your beliefs so you can build your expectations.

You can do it!

To wrap up this chapter and this book, I would like to say that <u>you can do it</u>. Everything that was discussed in this book is tools to equip you, the words to encourage you to achieve whatever your heart desires as a student and beyond. There is nothing you cannot be, have, or accomplish.

The bottom line is that it is up to you to get there. Yes, you will have some help and assistance along the way, but ultimately it is solely up to YOU.

Remember that you have the capacity and the power to make it happen. If at any time you feel discouraged, remember that you are the one. In fact, in those times, go back to the beginning of this chapter and review the affirmations you wrote under "I'm the One." I guarantee that after reading and reviewing them, you will develop a renewed strength that will keep you thriving.

My friend, now is the time… let's go get 'em.

Don't Give Up

Notes, Visions and Ideas

Made in United States
North Haven, CT
20 August 2024

56332331R00107